I Love

Bears

By Steve Parker
Illustrated by Andrea Morandi

Miles Kelly
PUBLISHING

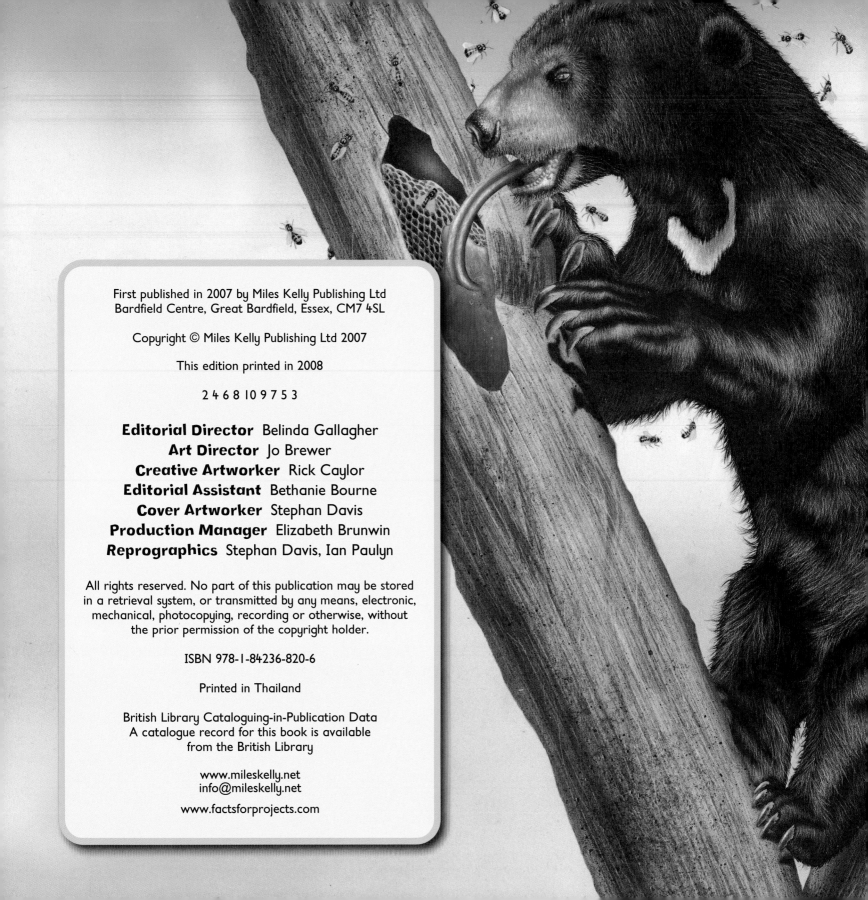

First published in 2007 by Miles Kelly Publishing Ltd
Bardfield Centre, Great Bardfield, Essex, CM7 4SL

Copyright © Miles Kelly Publishing Ltd 2007

This edition printed in 2008

2 4 6 8 10 9 7 5 3

Editorial Director Belinda Gallagher
Art Director Jo Brewer
Creative Artworker Rick Caylor
Editorial Assistant Bethanie Bourne
Cover Artworker Stephan Davis
Production Manager Elizabeth Brunwin
Reprographics Stephan Davis, Ian Paulyn

ISBN 978-1-84236-820-6

Printed in Thailand

British Library Cataloguing-in-Publication Data
A catalogue record for this book is available
from the British Library

www.mileskelly.net
info@mileskelly.net

www.factsforprojects.com

Contents

Kodiak bear

The biggest bear of all is the Kodiak bear. This huge brown bear can weigh almost one tonne — as much as a small car! It lives on Kodiak Island, in Alaska, North America.

The Kodiak bear lives in an area called its home range. It will leave smelly droppings in this area to warn other bears to stay away.

This bear has small front teeth for nibbling and nipping, and longer teeth for stabbing and tearing. Its back teeth are wide, for chewing.

Tall and small

A Kodiak bear may stand almost twice as high as a person — and weigh ten times as much.

The thick, furry coat helps to keep the Kodiak bear warm and dry — like a hairy raincoat!

Polar bear

The polar bear is one of the biggest bears, and it lives at the freezing North Pole. Polar bears are good swimmers. Baby polar bears are called cubs. They learn to swim by following their mother into the water.

Cubs are born in midwinter, in a den dug in the snow. They stay there with their mother for three months.

Thick fur and a layer of fat under its skin help to keep the polar bear warm in the icy sea.

The polar bear paddles through the water with its huge front paws. It can swim for many hours.

The polar bear cub learns to swim with its mother. Male bears never take part in caring for their cubs. In fact males may sometimes try to kill them.

Waiting for dinner

A polar bear may wait hours for a seal to visit its breathing hole. Then the bear grabs the seal as it surfaces.

Asian black bear

Most bears eat lots of different foods, including meat and plants. The Asian black bear loves nuts — beechnuts, hazelnuts, walnuts, chestnuts and pinenuts. However, sometimes this bear will eat farmers' crops such as sweetcorn.

The sweetcorn is torn off the stalk by the bear's long teeth.

Moon bear

The Asian black bear has a pale chest patch shaped like a half moon. This is why it is also known as the 'moon bear'.

The Asian black bear usually sleeps all day in a cave or a hollow tree. It comes out in the evening to look for food.

This bear can also be found in the Himalayan Mountains, where it is known as the Himalayan bear.

Sun bear

The sun bear is the smallest bear.
It is about the size of a big dog, but it
is much more powerful, with strong
muscles, sharp teeth and long claws.
It also has the shortest fur of any bear.
This bear loves honey so much, it is
sometimes called the 'honey bear'.

Long tongue
The sun bear's tongue can stretch 25 centimetres to lick food out of cracks. How long is your tongue?

Some bigger bears are too heavy to climb trees. The sun bear is light, and spends much of its time in the branches.

The bear's fur can be black, grey or brown. The round patch on its chest is orange or yellow – like the rising sun.

The bear tears open a bees' nest with its claws and quickly licks up the honey.

American black bear

A mother bear is huge, but her new cubs are tiny. When the newborn cubs of the American black bear are curled up asleep, each one is hardly bigger than your fist. Their eyes are closed, they cannot hear and they don't have much fur. When they get bigger, it is time to go outside.

The bears' den is in a cave or among the roots of a tree. The mother fills it with leaves so it is warm.

Bear legs!

Make a walking bear from pieces of card, fixed with split-pins so the legs move. Can it walk and wave at the same time?

The cubs stay near their mother for the first year of their lives. She protects them from danger, such as wolves and eagles.

The mother bear is quite shy. However, she will quickly get angry when protecting her cubs from danger.

Eurasian brown bear

The Eurasian brown bear lives across Europe and Asia. In the far north, where winters are long and cold, it sleeps for weeks on end. In warmer southern areas it sleeps much less.

This bear likes to sleep in a rocky cave, on a bed made from leaves and grass. It sleeps for up to six months.

Big foot
Bears leave tracks in snow, sand and mud. They are huge, each with a rounded paw and five long claws.

Giant panda

The giant panda is a very rare animal.
There are only about 1000 left living in the
wild, in China. This bear likes eating bamboo,
a type of woody grass. Sometimes the panda
will snack on different foods.

Six fingers?

The panda seems to have
six fingers. But the extra
one is really part of its
wrist. This helps it
to hold food.

A panda may steal
and eat eggs from a
bird's nest, but most
of its food is bamboo.

When it is born, a panda's fur is soft and fluffy. It soon becomes thick and rough to help keep the panda warm and dry.

Pandas prefer to stay near their mountaintop homes. They are shy animals and can be scared by people.

Brown bear

The brown bear is one of the biggest meat-eating land animals. As well as meat, it loves to eat fish, insects, birds' eggs, honey, fruit, berries — in fact, just about anything. The brown bear is always hungry!

After sleeping through the winter, the brown bear wakes up very hungry. It will eat all day long. Its favourite food is salmon.

Powerful legs mean that the brown bear can run fast when it is chasing prey.

This bear has a lump of muscle on its shoulders to give its front paws extra power and strength.

Grizzled grizzly
Brown bears are also called grizzlies. Their fur has white tips, making them look old, grey and 'grizzled'.

The brown bear catches salmon in its powerful jaws, or hooks them out of the water with its huge paws.

19

Sloth bear

Bears nearly always live alone, apart from a mother with her cubs. Sometimes sloth bears gather to share a big feast, such as juicy termites, or sweet, sticky honey in a bees' nest. After the meal, they wander off on their own again.

This bear's lips are strong, and it sucks up ants or termites one by one.

Hitch a ride!

The baby sloth bear rides on its mother's back. She has a special patch of fur for the baby to hang on to.

The sloth bear has long, shaggy fur. There is a white patch on its chest, often shaped like a Y or U.

The sloth bear is quite small, but its claws are very long. Each one is probably as big as your finger.

Spectacled bear

Of all the bears, the spectacled bear spends most of its time in trees. It climbs by wrapping its legs around the tree trunk and then it shuffles upwards. Pale-coloured fur around its eyes makes the bear look like it's wearing glasses!

Spectacled bears may build nests in trees to sleep in during the day.

Big-eyed bear
Each spectacled bear has its own shape of eye patches. No two are ever the same.

Bears often
stand up to look,
listen and sniff
for food or
danger.

The bear pulls down
low-growing branches
so it can eat the
fruits, or soft bark.

Fun facts

Kodiak bear Out of all the bears, the Kodiak bear is the largest.

Polar bear Lying in wait for a seal, a polar bear will try and cover its black nose with its paws so it cannot be seen.

Asian black bear These bears are very good climbers and like to rest in trees.

Sun bear The sun bear is also known as the dog bear and the honey bear.

American black bear Some American black bears can be brown, honey and even grey in colour.

Eurasian brown bear This bear is the smallest of all the brown bears.

Giant panda So they can eat their food more easily, giant pandas have an extra thumb.

Brown bear Female brown bears give birth to their babies while they are asleep.

Sloth bear The nostrils of the sloth bear can close. This stops ants crawling in.

Spectacled bear Though they are very good swimmers, the spectacled bear does not eat fish.